Scott Graham, Karl Hyde and Simon Stephens

Fatherland

G000066596

methuen | drama

LONDON · NEW YORK · OXFORD · NEW DELHI · SYDNEY

METHUEN DRAMA
Bloomsbury Publishing Plc
50 Bedford Square, London, WC1B 3DP, UK

First published in Great Britain by Methuen Drama 2017

New edition published 2018

Cover design: Olivia D'Cruz and Toby Way

Cover image © Perou

A catalogue record for this book is available from the British Library.

ISBN: PB: 978-1-3500-9150-4
ePDF: 978-1-3500-9151-1
eBook: 978-1-3500-9152-8

Series: Modern Plays

Typeset by Mark Heslington Ltd, Scarborough, North Yorkshire
Printed and bound in Great Britain

To find out more about our authors and books visit
www.bloomsbury.com and sign up for our *newsletters*.

Fatherland

by Scott Graham, Karl Hyde and Simon Stephens

Commissioned and produced by Lyric Hammersmith, Manchester International Festival, Frantic Assembly, the Royal Exchange Theatre and LIFT. Supported by PRS for Music Foundation.

Fatherland premiered at the Royal Exchange Theatre in July 2017 as part of Manchester International Festival before further performances in London at the Lyric Hammersmith as part of LIFT 2018.

Creative Team

Co-Author & Director	Scott Graham
Co-Author & Composer	Karl Hyde
Co-Author & Writer	Simon Stephens
Designer	Jon Bausor
Lighting Designer	Jon Clark
Co-Composer & Music Producer	Matthew Herbert
Sound Designer	Ian Dickinson for Autograph
Choreographer	Eddie Kay
Dramaturg	Nick Sidi
Vocal Coach	Beth Allen
Associate Musical Director/Vocal Coach	Kate Marlais
Casting Director	Will Burton CDG

Cast

Alan	Joseph Alessi
Karl	Mark Arends
Mel	Michael Begley
Scott	Declan Bennett
Martin (non-speaking role)	Luke Brown
Steve	James Doherty
Samir (non-speaking role)	Ankit Giri
Simon	Nyasha Hatendi
Daniel	David Judge
Graham	Neil McCaul
Craig	Tachia Newall
Jack (non-speaking role)	Luke Rigg
Luke	Craig Stein

Chorus of Others

Benjamin Aluwihare	Petros Dimotakis
Alex Ayliffe	Oz Direncay
Alessio Bagiardi	Tiarnan Doherty
Jack Bailey	Diogo Domingos
Joshua Alexander Barrow	Charles Entsie
Jamie Bell	Vaughan Evans
Punit Bhatia	Max George Ferguson
Sam Blake	Martin Fox
Youness Bouzinab	Colm Gallagher
Jono Clements	Michael Garbutt
Alexander Da Fonseca	Alexander Gauthier
Brian Daly	Alan Gill
Ritanjan Das	Sam Gladman
Gustavo Dias Ballejo	Elliot Graziano

Dominic Gregory
Craig Hamilton
Jonathon Hand
Tom Harrison
Mark Mo Haycox
Kaidyn Hinds
Joseph Honey
Ellis Hopkins
Oliver Jones
Luca Keaney
James Killeen
Matt Kyle
Yannis Lion
Anthony Mackey
Andrew Margerison
Andrew Maudie
Sean McAlinden Barber
Eoin McAndrew
James Gerard McKendrick
Craig McKenzie
Christopher McMullen
Geraldo Montero
Chris Moses
Cameron Muir
Timmy Neale
Chris Nikoloff
Nigel Oram

Robin Paley Yorke
Tyler Palo
Drew Paterson
Daniel Paul
Max Percy
Luis Perpetuo
Bailey Pilbean
Steven Pleasants
Callan Purcell
Nicholas Quirke
Iain Rankin
Dan Richard
Geoff Saunders
Douglas Simon
Nat Speight
Michael Spitzer
Garth Squance
Koray Thomasson
Callum Tickner
Aaron Tonks
Valeri Traykov
Mike Turner
Isaac Vincent
Daniel Walker
Elliot Weaver
Jake Webb
Douglas Wood

Production

Production Manager	Seamus Benson
Company Stage Manager	Claire Bryan
Deputy Stage Manager	Sarah Thomas
Assistant Stage Manager	Lucy Holland
Flying by Foy	

For Lyric Hammersmith

Artistic Director	Sean Holmes
Executive Director	Sian Alexander
Artistic Associates	Jude Christian, Paule Constable, Joel Horwood, Ola Ince, Ferdy Roberts, Tal Rosner
Head of Production	Seamus Benson
Director of Development	Lucy Howe
Senior Producer	Imogen Kinchin

Senior Producer	Mimi Poskitt
Director of Young People	Nicholai La Barrie
Director of Finance and Resources	Louise Zandstra
Producer	Peter Holland
Assistant Producer	Sarah Georgeson

For Frantic Assembly

Artistic Director	Scott Graham
Executive Director	Kerry Whelan
Producer	Peter Holland
Associate Director	Neil Bettles
Head of Learning & Participation	Sharon Kanolik
General Manager	Angie Fullman
Associate Director (Learn & Train)	Simon Pittman
Learn & Participation Coordinator	Juliet Styles
Finance and Office Administrator	Gemma Grand

For Manchester International Festival

CEO & Artistic Director	John McGrath
Managing Director	Christine Cort
Executive Director	Fiona Gasper
Executive Producer	Jo Paton
Executive Producer	Kate Mackonochie
Production Administrator	Hannah Clapham-Clark
Co-Commissioning Administrator	Hannah Falvey
Creative Learning Director	Jennifer Cleary
Creative Learning Director (Maternity Cover)	Julia Turpin
Creative Learning Manager	Sarah Hiscock
Casting Associate*	Anne McNulty CDG

*Consultant

For Royal Exchange Theatre

Artistic Director	Sarah Frankcom
Executive Director	Mark Dobson
Associate Artistic Directors	Amit Sharma, Matthew Xia
Associate Artists	Maxine Peake, Benji Reid, Chris Thorpe
Development Director	Val Young
Director of Finance and Administration	Barry James
Operations Director	Jo Topping
Director of Marketing and Communications	Claire Will

Senior Producer	Ric Watts
Creative Learning and Engagement Interim Manager	Chris Wright
Head of Production	Simon Curtis
Consultant Producer	Richard Morgan

For LIFT

Artistic Director & Joint CEO	Kris Nelson
Guest Artistic Director, LIFT 2018	David Binder
Executive Director & Joint CEO	Beki Bateson
Senior Producer	Carolyn Forsyth
Senior Producer	Jon Davis
Partnerships & Development Manager	Francis Christeller
Development Assistant	Cameron Henderson-Begg
Head of Finance and Operations	David Lewis
Finance & Operations Manager	Dan Jacques
Projects Manager	Priya Jethwa
Head of Marketing & Digital	Bonnie Smith
Marketing & Digital Coordinator	Maya Ophelia
Production Managers	Mekel Edwards and Simon MacColl
Projects Assistant	Patricia Akoli

Thanks to:

Mike Gillespie and Anis Marks at
The Sunday Club
Mel Kenyon
Sean Hollands
Christine Gettins
Lisa Maguire
Despina Tsatsas

Alex Glaysher
James Wedlock
Finnan Twigg
Sian Graham
David Teasdale
Jennie Price

And all the people who so generously contributed their stories

Supported using public funding by **ARTS COUNCIL ENGLAND** LOTTERY FUNDED

The Lyric Hammersmith is one of the UK's leading producing theatres. For more than one hundred and twenty years it has been responsible for creating some of the UK's most adventurous and acclaimed theatrical work. It has gained a national reputation for its work with and for children and young people and creates pathways into the arts for young talent from all backgrounds, helping to diversify our industry. Recent productions include our critically acclaimed annual pantomimes, the smash hit *Bugsy Malone*, the international tour and co-production with Filter Theatre of *A Midsummer Night's Dream* and the UK premiere of the international phenomenon *Terror*.

The Lyric's dual commitment to producing the highest quality contemporary theatre alongside nurturing the creativity of young people is what make it unique within the cultural ecology of the UK. It is a local theatre rooted in its community with a national and international reputation for the quality and innovation of its artistic work.

In April 2015 the Lyric reopened following a multi-million pound capital project, which saw the addition of the Reuben Foundation Wing housing state-of-the-art facilities for theatre, dance, film, music, digital and more. The 'new' Lyric is now the largest creative hub in West London and home to an innovative partnership of like-minded leading arts organisations who work together to deliver life-changing creative opportunities for thousands of young West Londoners.

Artistic Director **Sean Holmes**

Executive Director **Sian Alexander**

For more information, please visit **lyric.co.uk**

Supported by

Registered Charity, No. 278518

FRANTIC ASSEMBLY

Award-winning theatre company Frantic Assembly's method of devising theatre has been impacting on theatrical practice and unlocking the creative potential of future theatre-makers for up to 23 years.

One of the most exciting theatre companies in the UK, Frantic Assembly is led by Artistic Director and co-founder Scott Graham, has toured extensively across Great Britain, and worked in 40 countries internationally collaborating with some of today's most inspiring artists.

Frantic Assembly is currently studied as leading contemporary theatre practitioners on five British and international academic syllabuses. The success of the company's distinct approach has influenced contemporary theatre-making and foregrounded the use of movement directors and choreographers in new dramatic works. With a history of commissioning writers such as Mark Ravenhill, Abi Morgan, Simon Stephens and Bryony Lavery the company has been acclaimed for its collaborative approach. In 2016 the company started delivering practical modules on a new Collaborative Theatre-Making MA it has created with Coventry University (UK Modern University of the Year 2014, 2015, 2016 and UK University of the Year 2015). Frantic Assembly runs Ignition, a free national training programme for young men aged 16–20, increasing involvement in and access to the arts in places of low cultural engagement.

Frantic Assembly productions include *Fatherland*, *Things I Know to Be True* (UK and Australia), *Othello*, *Beautiful Burnout* (UK, Australia, New Zealand and New York), *Lovesong*, *Stockholm* (UK and Australia), *The Believers*. They are also the Movement Directors on the award-winning National Theatre of Great Britain production *The Curious Incident of the Dog in the Night-Time* (West End, Broadway, UK & Ireland tour, US tour). Television credits include Movement Direction on BAFTA-winning British – American series *Humans* (AMC, Channel 4 & Kudos).

Registered Charity Number: 1113716

Facebook @franticassembly

Twitter @franticassembly

Instagram frantic_assembly

Youtube franticassembly

Manchester International Festival (MIF) is the world's first festival of original, new work and special events, staged every two years in Manchester, UK. MIF launched in 2007 as an artist-led festival, presenting new works from across the spectrum of performing arts, visual arts and popular culture.

MIF has commissioned, produced and presented world premieres by artists including **Björk, Steve McQueen, Robert Wilson, Sharmeen Obaid-Chinoy, Jeremy Deller, Wayne McGregor, Maxine Peake, Boris Charmatz, The xx, Zaha Hadid Architects, Thomas Ostermeier, Damon Albarn, Punchdrunk, Elbow** and **Marina Abramović.**

MIF brings together world-renowned artists from different art forms and backgrounds to create dynamic, innovative and forward-thinking new work, staged in venues across Greater Manchester – from theatres, galleries and concert halls to railway depots, churches and car parks. MIF works closely with venues, festivals and other cultural organisations globally, whose financial and creative input helps to make many of these projects possible and ensures that work made at MIF goes on to be seen around the world. MIF is also working across Manchester through My Festival – a lively community of creative people of all ages and backgrounds from every corner of the city – forging closer connections and opening up new creative opportunities in local neighbourhoods.

MIF's Artistic Director and CEO is John McGrath. Planning is now underway for MIF19, which will take place 4–21 July 2019 and will bring extraordinary commissions from across the world. MIF is also set to manage and lead the artistic programme for The Factory, a new £110 million cultural centre in Manchester, which is due to open in 2020.

MIF is a registered charity and company limited by guarantee.

mif.co.uk

Manchester's Royal Exchange Theatre Company transforms the way people see theatre, each other and the world around them.

Their historic building, once the world's biggest cotton exchange, was taken over by artists in 1976. Today it is an award-winning cultural charity that produces new theatre in-the-round, in communities, on the road and online.

Exchange remains at the heart of everything they make and do. Now their currency is brand new drama and reinvigorated classics, the boldest artists and a company of highly skilled makers – all brought together to trade ideas and experiences with the people of Greater Manchester (and beyond).

The Exchange's unique auditorium is powerfully democratic, a space where audiences and performers meet as equals, entering and exiting through the same doors. It is the inspiration for all they do; inviting everyone to understand the past, engage in today's big questions, collectively imagine a better future and lose themselves in the moment of a great night out.

Their Spring Summer 2018 season includes stories from an incredible array of artists, including Associate Artists RashDash, alongside Maxine Peake, as writer and performer, Sarah Frankcom, Bryony Shanahan, Michael Boyd and new partners Yellow Earth – all using their distinctive performance styles in a season that brings us all together for a live experience, and asks us to look again at the world in which we live.

royalexchange.co.uk

Registered charity no.255424

twitter @rxtheatre

instagram.com/rxtheatre

facebook.com/rxtheatre

youtube.com/rxtheatre

LIFT travels the world to bring global stories to London, creating spectacular performances and moments of magic in every corner of the Capital. For nearly 40 years it has presented shows in partnership with London's major arts venues, theatres and galleries, but also in countless hidden spaces and places across the city. It works with world-class artists, whose radical imaginations create exceptional work that questions the nature of theatre, engages with the big ideas of our time, and reveals the stories and communities of our incredibly diverse Capital.

Alongside LIFT's biennial London-wide festival sits a programme of year-round activity that includes large scale projects, artist residencies, national touring and its ground-breaking participatory work, LIFT Tottenham.

In recent years LIFT has commissioned over 40 new productions and events from around the world including *Minefield* (Lola Arias, LIFT 2016 and 2017/18 UK tour), *Depart* (Circa, LIFT 2016 and 2017 UK tour), *Phaedra(s)* (Odéon–Théâtre de l'Europe, LIFT 2016), *Absent* (dreamthinkspeak, 2015), *The Notebook* (Forced Entertainment, LIFT 2014), *Symphony of a Missing Room* (Lundahl & Seitl, LIFT 2014) and *Deblozay* (Rara Woulib, LIFT 2014).

liftfestival.com

Biographies

Creative Team

Scott Graham | Co-Author & Director

Scott is Artistic Director/co-founder of Frantic Assembly. Directing credits include *Fatherland*, *Things I Know to Be True*, *No Way Back*, *Othello* (TMA Award for Best Direction)*, The Believers*. Co-directing credits include *Little Dogs*, *Lovesong*, *Beautiful Burnout* (Drama Desk nomination)*, Stockholm*, *pool (no water)*, *Dirty Wonderland*. He was nominated for an Olivier and a Tony Award for Best Choreography on the National Theatre production *The Curious Incident of the Dog in the Night-Time*. He also directed *Home* for the National Theatre of Scotland. Choreography/movement direction includes *Husbands & Sons*, *Port*, *The Hothouse* and *Market Boy* for the National Theatre; *The Merchant of Venice* for Singapore Repertory Company; *Praxis Makes Perfect* for National Theatre Wales; *The Canticles* at Brighton Festival/Aldeburgh Music; *Dr Dee* for Manchester International Festival/ENO.

He has, with Steven Hoggett, written *The Frantic Assembly Book of Devising Theatre* and is Visiting Professor in Theatre Practice at Coventry University.

Karl Hyde | Co-Author & Composer

Karl studied fine art at Stourbridge and Cardiff, co-founded Underworld and the art collective Tomato, recording and performing live since 1968, occasionally collaborating with Brian Eno. He has exhibited artworks internationally since 1978, and published the books *Mmm Skyscraper I love You*, *In the Belly of St Paul*, *I am Dogboy*. Film and theatre credits (as Underworld) include *Beautiful Burnout* (National Theatre of Scotland/Frantic Assembly); *Frankenstein* (National Theatre, Olivier nominated), *Trainspotting*, *A Life Less Ordinary*, *Sunshine* (all dir. Danny Boyle); *Breaking & Entering* (dir. Anthony Minghella). In 2012 Underworld were musical directors of the London Summer olympics opening ceremony. In 2016 Underworld's *Barbara Barbara*, *We Face a Shining Future* was nominated for a Grammy.

In 2017, Karl and Underworld partner Rick Smith presented *Manchester Street Poem*, at Manchester International Festival, a performed installation bringing attention to the stories of those who find themselves homeless in the city.

Simon Stephens | Co-Author & Writer

Simon's plays have been translated into more than thirty languages and performed throughout the world for two decades. He has won many awards including two Olivier Awards and a Tony Award for Best New Play. He is an Artistic Associate at the Lyric Hammersmith and Associate Playwright at the Royal Court Theatre. He is a Professor of Scriptwriting at Manchester Metropolitan University and a Fellow of Royal Welsh College of Music and Drama.

His plays include: *Punk Rock*, *A Thousand Stars Explode in the Sky*, *Three Kingdoms*, *Morning* and a new version of *The Seagull*, all of which premiered at the Lyric Hammersmith.

Jon Bausor | Designer

Jon studied at Oxford University and Motley Theatre Design Course. He designed the London 2012 Paralympics Opening Ceremony.

As an associate artist of the Royal Shakespeare Company, he has designed numerous productions, including *Hamlet*, *King Lear*, *The Winter's Tale* and the entire 2012 'What Country Friends Is This?' season.

Other theatre includes: *Bat Out of Hell* (Manchester/Coliseum/ Dominion Theatre); *The Grinning Man* (Bristol Old Vic/Trafalgar Studios, Best Design – UK Theatre Awards); *The James Plays* (both English and Scottish National Theatres/world tour); *Kursk* (Sound&Fury, Young Vic, Sydney Opera House); *Ghost Stories* (West End/Toronto, Moscow); *Peter Pan*, *Lord of the Flies* (Regent's Park Open Air Theatre); *Mametz* (National Theatre Wales; Best Design – UK Theatre and Wales Theatre Awards); *The Believers* (Frantic Assembly); *You for Me for You* (Royal Court); *I Am Yusuf* (Shibahurr, Palestine/ Young Vic); *The Plough and the Stars* (Abbey Theatre, Dublin/US tour).

Dance and opera include: *The Nutcracker*, *Carmen* (Norwegian National Opera and Ballet); *Hansel and Gretel*, *Ghosts*, *Pleasure's Progress* (Royal Opera House); *In Medias Res* (Nederlands Dans Theater); *Lest We Forget* (English National Ballet).

Jon Clark | Lighting Designer

Jon has designed extensively for the National Theatre, the Royal Shakespeare Company, Young Vic, Almeida Theatre, Donmar Warehouse, Lyric Hammersmith, in the West End, on Broadway and with many other companies internationally. He has been twice nominated for the Olivier Awards and is the recipient of a Green Room Award and Knight of Illumination Award.

Recent designs for theatre include: *The Inheritance* and *The Jungle* (Young Vic); *Amadeus* and *Absolute Hell* (National Theatre).

Recent designs for opera include: *The Exterminating Angel* (Metropolitan Opera, Royal Opera House, Salzburg Festival, Royal Danish Opera); *Lucia Di Lammermoor*, *Krol Roger, Written on Skin* (Royal Opera House).

Matthew Herbert | Co-Composer & Music Producer

Matthew is a composer, artist and writer whose work spans music, film, the stage, gallery and radio. His primary medium is sound and he is perhaps best known for his use of 'found sound' in his process.

Theatre credits include: *People, Places and Things* (Headlong/ National Theatre), *Edgar & Annabel* (National Theatre), *Machinal* (Broadway).

Film credits include: *Life in a Day*, *Fantastic Woman*, *Disobedience*.

Music credits (beyond his own artist work) include: Quincy Jones, Serge Gainsbourg, Ennio Morricone, Björk and Dizzee Rascal.

Writer credits include: *The Hush* (National Theatre) and *The Crackle* (Royal Opera House).

Ian Dickinson for Autograph | Sound Designer

Ian is a UK-based sound designer with extensive domestic and international credits to his name. Recent shows include *Hangmen* and *Angels in America*, both in New York; Most notably, he received an Olivier Award for *The Curious Incident of the Dog in the Night-Time* which has since been critically acclaimed around the world.

Ian has been a member of the Autograph design team since 2009.

For more information visit *www.autograph.co.uk*

Eddie Kay | Choreographer

Eddie is a movement director who studied at London Contemporary Dance School and Northern School of Contemporary Dance.

Dance and theatre include: *Katie Roche*, *Ulysses*, *The Unmanageable Sisters* (Abbey Theatre); *The Blue Boy*, *This Beach* (Brokentalkers); *Fatherland* (Frantic Assembly and Manchester International Festival); *The Pass*, *You for Me for You* (Royal Court); *All's Well that Ends Well* (Shakespeare's Globe); *Brave New World* (Royal & Derngate); *Scuttlers* (Manchester Royal Exchange); *The Radicalisation of Bradley Manning* (National Theatre Wales); *Romeo and Juliet* (West Yorkshire Playhouse); *Kite* (Wrong Crowd); *Bromance* (BMT); *The 306: Dawn* (NTS).

He has performed for Frantic Assembly in *Hymns*, *Dirty Wonderland*, *Othello*, *Beautiful Burnout*.

Nick Sidi | Dramaturg

Nick is a dramaturg, actor and producer.

As an actor Nick has numerous television and film credits. On stage, he has appeared at the National Theatre, the Royal Court, the Young Vic, the Royal Exchange Theatre and in the West End. He has collaborated regularly with Simon Stephens, appearing in five of his plays.

As a dramaturg, Nick assisted Simon Stephens on *Song from Far Away* (Young Vic) and Lindsey Ferrentino on *Amy and the Orphans* (Roundabout, New York), and has worked as part of the National Theatre New Writing Department.

In 2016, he became Associate Producer of Elliott & Harper Productions, where he is responsible for developing the company's slate of new writing.

Beth Allen | Vocal Coach

Beth is a classically trained opera singer, qualified music therapist and spoken voice coach for theatre with an MA in Voice. Her work life equally balances creativity with therapy. She has been a television presenter/singer for thirty programmes for the BBC (*What? Where? When? Why?*) and choral director for three consecutive Manchester

International Festival productions including Sir John Tavener's *If Ye Love Me* at Bridgewater Hall, *Neck of the Woods* at HOME and *Fatherland* at the Royal Exchange. She also coached the award-winning chorus for *Suppliant Women* at the Royal Exchange.

Kate Marlais | Associate Musical Director/Vocal Coach

Kate studied Music with a Composition major at King's College London. Having also studied classical singing, she then trained in musical theatre at the Royal Academy of Music.

As performer, credits include *War Horse* (West End) and *The Human Comedy* (Young Vic).

Kate is Resident Composer at Lyric Hammersmith. She is Associate of the Royal Academy of Music (ARAM), awarded for her work in music. As co-writer/composer, she won the S&S Award for musical *HERE*, in conjunction with Curve Leicester and Mercury Musical Developments.

Kate also worked on *Fatherland* (Manchester Royal Exchange) for Manchester International Festival.

Cast

Joseph Alessi | Alan

Theatre credits include: *Fatherland* (Manchester Royal Exchange, Manchester International Festival 2017); *The Lorax* (Old Vic/Toronto); *The Plague* (Arcola); *Adding Machine* (Finborough); *Monster Raving Loony* (Drum/Soho); *The One That Got Away* (Ustinov); *The Hook* (Liverpool Everyman); *A Midsummer Night's Dream* (Royal & Derngate); *Brief Encounter* (Kneehigh/UK, US, Australian tours/Studio 54, Broadway); *Tartuffe* (Liverpool Playhouse/ETT UK tour); *Absurd Person Singular* (Curve); *Privates on Parade* (West Yorkshire Playhouse/Birmingham Rep); *The Drowsy Chaperone* (Novello); *Antony and Cleopatra*, *Julius Caesar*, *The Tempest* (RSC/Novello/USA tour); *The Postman Always Rings Twice* (West Yorkshire Playhouse/Playhouse); *The Play Wot I Wrote* (UK tour); *Light* (Complicite/Almeida/UK tour); *The Colour of Justice – The Stephen Lawrence enquiry* (Tricycle); *Animal Crackers* (Royal Exchange/UK tour/Barbican/West End).

Mark Arends | Karl

Theatre credits include: *Old Fools* (Southwark Playhouse); *The Missing Light* (Old Vic); *Hamlet* (Trafalgar Studios); *Don't Sleep There Are Snakes* (Park Theatre); *The Angry Brigade* (Bush); *The Two Gentlemen of Verona* (RSC); *1984*, *Marianne Dreams* (Almeida); *Beauty and the Beast*, *A Dream Play*, *The Cat in the Hat*, *The UN Inspector* (National Theatre); *Love's Comedy*, *Alison's House* (Orange Tree); *Macbeth*, *The May Queen*, *Urban Legend* (Liverpool Everyman); *The Glass Menagerie*, *Henry V*, *What Every Woman Knows* (Manchester Royal Exchange); *Something Very Far Away* (Unicorn).

Film and television credits include: *New Tricks*, *Doctors*, *Skins*, *The Innocence Project*, *Silent Witness*, *The Bill*, *Casualty*, *Holby City*, *Draw On Sweet Night*, *Pride and Prejudice*.

Michael Begley | Mel

Theatre credits include: *Matilda* (RSC); *After Electra* (Tricycle/Theatre Royal Plymouth); *The Glass Supper* (Hampstead); *Mrs Lowry and Son* (Trafalgar Studios); *Sweet Bird of Youth* (Old Vic); *If There Is I Haven't Found It Yet* (Bush); *Rhinoceros*, *The Arsonists* (Royal Court); *Who's*

Afraid of Virginia Woolf (Royal Exchange); *Martha Loves Michael* (Ruffian/Pleasance); *The Norman Conquests* (Birmingham Rep); *Hobson's Choice* (Touring Consortium/Birmingham Rep/Plymouth Theatre Royal); *Death of a Salesman*, *Life of Galileo* (Library); *Hunting Scenes from Lower Bavaria* (Gate).

Television credits include: *Foyle's War*, *Dr Who*, *Miss Marple*, *William and Mary*, *Bob and Rose*, *City Central*, *McLibel!*, *This Life*, *Hillsborough.*

Film credits include: *Vacuuming Completely Nude in Paradise.*

Declan Bennett | Scott

Theatre credits include: *Kiss of the Spider Woman* (Menier Chocolate Factory); *Jesus Christ Superstar* (Regent's Park Open Air Theatre); *Once* (Phoenix); *American Idiot* (St. James Theatre/Broadway); *Rent* (Nederlander Theatre/Broadway/US national tour); *Taboo* (The Venue/ UK tour); *The Kissing Dance* (Edinburgh Festival/UK tour); *It's a Lovely Day Tomorrow*, *Our Day Out* (Belgrade).

Television credits include: *EastEnders.*

Film credits include: *Inside Llewyn Davis*, *Contagion.*

Luke Brown | Martin

Performance credits include: *The Dandelion Child* (Tobacco Factory); *Fatherland* (Manchester Royal Exchange, Manchester International Festival 2017); *The Hotel Experience* (The Point, Eastleigh/Gulbenkian, University of Kent/Chichester University); *For You I Long the Longest* (Swindon Dance Theatre, The Point Eastleigh, Newbury Corn Exchange/Marine Theatre/South Hill Park); *Us* (Norwich and Norfolk Outdoor Festival, Eastleigh Unwrapped at The Point, Out There Festival Great Yarmouth); *Marble and Bread* (The Sailors House Limerick); *The Perfect American Opera* (English National Opera/Opera Queensland); *Spectrum* (The Point, Eastleigh).

Film credits include: *The Reunion.*

James Doherty | Steve

Theatre credits include: *London Road*, *National Theatre: 50 Years on Stage*, *Beyond Caring* (National Theatre); *Eventide* (Arcola); *Chicago*

(Garrick); *Marguerite* (Theatre Royal Haymarket); *Les Misérables* (Palace Theatre); *Kiss Me Kate* (Royal Albert Hall).

Television credits include: *The Windsors, Veep, The Thick of It, Him & Her the Wedding, Rev, Miranda, The IT Crowd, Delicious, Cradle to the Grave, The Job Lot, Phoneshop, Count Arthur Strong, Touch of Cloth, Mongrels, Todd Margaret, Watson & Oliver, Endeavour, Ambassadors, The Jury, The Royal, Peak Practice, Eastenders, Coronation Street, Waterloo Road, Casualty, Holby City, 2.4 Children,The Wyvern Mystery.*

Film credits include: *London Road, In the Loop, Closed Circuit, Backbeat.*

Ankit Giri | Samir

Ankit Giri graduated from East15 Acting School in 2017.

Theatre credits include: *Fatherland* (Manchester Royal Exchange, Manchester International Festival 2017); *Pericles* (Cornucopia).

Nyasha Hatendi | Simon

For the Lyric: *The Resistible Rise of Arturo UI*.

Theatre credits include: *King Charles III* (Music Box Theatre/Almedia); *Richard III* (Nottingham Playhouse/York Theatre Royal); *NHAMO* (Tiata Fahodzhi/Tricycle); *'Tis Pity She's a Whore* (Cheek By Jowl); *11 and 12* (Théâtre des Bouffe du Nord); *The Brother's Size* (ATC/Young Vic); *Pericles, The Winter's Tale* (RSC); *As You Like It* (Theatre Royal Bath)

Film credits include: *The Frontrunner, Replicas, Narcopolis, The Comedian, The Ghost Writer, The Good Shepherd.*

Television credits include: *The Forgiving Earth, Casual, W1A, Strikeback, Garrow's Law, Blood and Oil, The No.1 Ladies' Detectives Agency.*

David Judge | Daniel

For the Lyric: *Three Sisters*

Theatre credits include: *The Kitchen Sink* (Oldham Coliseum); *The Caretaker* (Bristol Old Vic/Royal & Derngate); *Fatherland* (Manchester Royal Exchange, Manchester International Festival 2017); *Scuttlers*,

Christmas Is Miles Away (Manchester Royal Exchange); *Statements* (Jermyn Street); *Schoolboy/Lover* (West Yorkshire Playhouse); *Scrappers* (Liverpool Playhouse); *A Taste of Honey* (Sheffield Crucible); *Northern Spirit* (Northern Stage); *Coming Home, Afterbirth* (Arcola); *Irish Pele, Crying in the Chapel* (Manchester Contact Theatre); *The Eleventh Capital* (Royal Court); *The Rise and Fall of Little Voice* (Harrogate Theatre); *An Argument About Sex* (Tramway/Traverse).

Television and film credits include: *Prey, Casualty, The Bill, Hollyoaks, The Omid Djalili Show, New Street Law, Silent Witness, An American Haunting.*

Neil McCaul | Graham

Recent theatre credits include: *Fatherland* (Manchester Royal Exchange, Manchester International Festival 2017); *After Electra* (Theatre Royal Plymouth/Tricycle); *Guys and Dolls* (Chichester/Savoy); *A Life*; *The Drawer Boy* (Finborough); *Twelfth Night* (Singapore Repertory Theatre); *A Round Heeled Woman* (Riverside Studios/ Aldwych); *Fings Ain't Wot They Used to Be* (Union); *Little Voice* (Hull); *Oedipus* (National Theatre); *Chicago* (Adelphi); *Brighton Rock* (Almeida).

Film credits include: *The Lion* (YouTube); *Speed Love, Pleasure Island, In Love with Alma Cogan*; *Billy the Kid & The Green Baize Vampire*; *The Pirates of Penzance.*

Television credits include: *Benidorm, Midsomer Murders, Foyle's War, Doctors, Holby City.*

Tachia Newall | Craig

Theatre credits include: *Scuttlers* (Royal Exchange); *Fatherland* (Manchester Royal Exchange, Manchester International Festival 2017); *Hamlet, Hoax: My Lonely Heart* (Royal Exchange); *Some Like It Hip Hop* (Sadler's Wells); *Arabian Nights, The Manchester Lines* (Library); *Aladdin* (Preston Charter Theatre); *Crystal Kisses* (Contact); *Aladdin* (Imagine); *Ghost Boy* (20 Stories High).

Television credits include: *Silent Witness, From Darkness, Vera, Scott and Bailey, Casualty, Waterloo Road, Coronation Street, Young Dracula, Doctors, Moving On.*

Film credits include: *Dirty God.*

Luke Rigg | Jack

Performance credits include: *Fatherland* (Manchester Royal Exchange, Manchester International Festival 2017); *Trapped* (Experiential, tour); 5 Soldiers (Rosie Kay Dance, tour); *Bounce* (Harnisch Lacey, tour); *Milk Night* (Frantic Assembly, tour); *Lucid Grounds*, *Two Old Men*, *Out of His Skin*, *7.0*, *Subterania* (2Faced Dance, tour); *Stags* (Citrus Arts, tour).

Film credits include: *Coded Dreams*, *Kill Me If You Can* (Channel 4)

Craig Stein | Luke

Theatre credits include: *Wig Out*, *FELA!*, *Nation* (National Theatre); *Doctor Faustus* (Duke of York's), *Neighbours* (HighTide/Nuffield); *Ghost* (Piccadilly); *5, 6, 7, 8* (Royal Court/Rough Cuts); *The Harder They Come* (Nottingham Playhouse/UK tour); *Wicked* (Apollo Victoria).

Film and television credits include: *Lake Placid: Legacy*, *Mary Poppins Returns*, *Soft Lad*, *Doctors*, *Song from Jenny*, *Law and Order*, *Love Matters: Aphrodite Fry*, *Holby City*, *Down to Earth*, *The Biz!*, *Casualty.*

Fatherland

Characters

Scott
Luke
Simon
Karl
Graham
Alan
Steve
Mel
Daniel
Craig

Scott Do you know anything about what we're doing?

Luke Erm my friend just said you're devising a show called *Fatherland*, is it? To do with fathers, sons and family, can you turn up?

Simon So um, so do you know anything about who we are?

Luke Yeah.

Scott Yeah?

Luke Erm I've seen some of the Frantic Assembly shows and . . .

Scott Oh cool.

Luke . . . saw *Beautiful Burnout* when it was here.

Simon Great.

Luke Yeah and I really enjoyed that show.

Scott Great.

Simon Yeah.

Luke Yeah. And I saw *Trainspotting*. Obviously! My dad showed it me, actually.

Karl Excellent.

Luke They had that *Curious Incident* thing on NT Live here.

Simon Yeah?

Luke But I didn't see that.

Simon No.

Scott Yeah so we are erm sorry, I'm not doing my emails I'm trying to find an image for you and I'm struggling erm . . .

Simon What's the image of?

Scott Do you know the erm . . .

Luke   It's very tense.

Scott   Remember I showed you that image about how I like to make the show and how I consider the interviews to be like a patchwork where the . . .

Simon   Yes very good.

Scott   Erm . . .

Karl   Have you found it?

Scott   Yes I think I have.

Karl   Well done.

Scott   So erm anyway so what I want to do with this idea is to make a show about erm fatherhood and just looking at vast experiences, understandings . . .

Luke   Mm.

Simon   . . . and expectations . . .

Scott   Yeah. Expectations . . . of what that is.

Simon   Yes.

Scott   And we have identified erm this process of just getting out there and meeting people and talking to people about their experiences because their experiences will go beyond ours. And you don't have to have the most extreme experiences, just meeting anybody new will open up our imagination.

Simon   Exactly.

Luke   Mm. Right.

Scott   Erm, and Karl can record it as well if that's all right with you?

Luke   Yeah.

Scott   Erm and because of that what I'll need to do is get you to sign . . .

Luke Yeah.

Scott . . . erm just there. So have a little read but also we're gonna be sticking one of these little microphones on you so you're gonna be very famous for an hour.

Luke It's what I've always wanted.

Karl Great erm okay so. Would you be able to clip that on for us?

Luke All right I . . . I've never worn a microphone so . . .

Karl Okay just, let's see . . . So this is a miniature lavalier from Sennheiser. It's directional.

Luke Put it on the shirt collar?

Karl Is that all right there?

Luke Yeah that's good now. Yeah thanks.

Scott Okay. Is that all right?

Luke Thank you. Yeah that's great.

Scott Erm so, what . . . this is . . . this is day one, you know.

Luke Mm mm.

Scott We decided to go back to each of our hometowns.

Simon Yeah.

Scott And interview people. Erm so we go from Corby coz this is where I'm from to Stockport where Simon's from . . .

Luke Mm.

Scott And then to Kidderminster where Karl grew up.

Luke Stockport yeah?

Scott Our glamorous hometowns.

Karl Sorry, Luke, can you count?

Luke Aye?

Karl   Into the microphone

Luke   1, 2, 3, 4, 5 . . .

Karl   Thank you.

Scott   Erm and each person we interview it's just of course one person, one experience and we're . . .

Luke   Mm.

Scott   . . . gonna build up a picture of the greater experience . . .

Luke   Yeah.

Scott   . . . by kind of collecting all of those. To make something big out of many little fragments. Erm and it's partly inspired by this painting erm which is a Salvador Dali painting.

Simon   'Gala Contemplating the Mediterranean Sea which at Twenty Meters Becomes the Portrait of Abraham Lincoln'.

Luke   Mm mm.

Scott   The way the tiny fragments of this painting go together to make something bigger. Because that's what we're hoping each individual, individual, individual –

Simon   Shard.

Scott   Yes, shard, will do. Go together to make something bigger. So Simon's gonna lead on the interview and erm it's based on a load of questions that he's created that we actually tried out on each other.

Luke   Okay.

Simon   What's your name?
How old are you?
Where are you from?
What did your father look like?
What kind of clothes do you remember him wearing?
What pastimes did he have?

What type of music did your dad like?
What job did he do?
Did he ever talk about his job with you?
Did he ever take you to his workplace?
Did your friends ever meet your dad? What did they think of him?
Did he ever talk about sex with you?
Did he ever talk about love with you?
What do you think attracted him to your mother?
What do you think attracted your mother to him?
Did he ever discipline you?
In what way?
Do you still see him now?
What's the earliest memory of your father?

Karl   Have you turned your phone off? Erm.

Luke   My phone's off.

Karl   Is it completely off, not just on silent?

Scott   Okay and do you mind if we take photos as well?

Luke   No I don't mind. No.

Simon   So erm . . . just for the . . . just for the recording. Just erm what, just tell us your full name?

Luke   Luke Hatton.

Graham   Graham Hyde.

Alan   Alan Hall. H.A.L.L.

Steve   Steve Leigh.

Mel   Er yeah, my name is Mel Turbott.

Daniel   Daniel Holley.

Craig   Craig Mutch.

Simon   How old are you, Craig?

Craig   I am thirty-four. Thirty-five, actually.

Simon   And you're from Corby?

Craig   I'm from Corby, born in Corby, yeah.

Simon   And, and lived here all your life?

Craig   All, all my life, yeah. So, yeah, never, never left. Ah, always thought about it but just never got there. So . . .

Simon   And how many children have you got?

Craig   I've got two children, Daisy Mae who's ten and Lottie who's four.

Simon   And, ah, what's the earliest memory of your father?

Craig   I've never, er.

I never met him.

My dad was married to somebody else when he got my mum pregnant. My mum's never really filled me in with the whole story, so it's not something we've really got a connection about. She's told me bits and bobs. I've never really pushed her. She was sixteen. I think he was twenty-three. She'd be hanging outside the pub looking through the window at him. So, eventually they must have got together in a one-night bunk-up or whatever but she's never told me. She's the one who said, oh, your dad was my first love but . . . well, I don't think it was reciprocated.

So, she's seventeen by the time she had me, sixteen when she fell pregnant.

He, he was just a young lad looking for a young girl on the go. So, I was born nine months later. Ah, my grandad raised me . . . My nana and my grandad. My mum was still living at home with grandad and nana.

Is this all right?

Scott   He's very nervous. Craig. He rang me at about 11 o'clock last night.

Simon   Nervous?

Scott   I think he'd been drinking. He said he'd not slept for a few days thinking about it.

Simon   Fuck.

Scott   I know.

Simon   Why?

Scott   I don't know.

I'll tell you who won't be nervous. Alan.

Simon   Who's Alan?

Scott   He's one of the boys who's coming in.

He was a bit of a one.

Simon   A bit of a one?

Scott   He was very, very violent. He's a bit of a psychopath.

Karl   Excellent.

Scott   A right violent bastard.

Simon   And he's coming in tomorrow?

Scott   He used to terrify me. He used to terrify all of us.

Alan   I've never even been in a effing theatre before.

Simon   Right.

Alan   Theatres like one of them things like, you know, it's just, you know.

Simon   Yeah.

Alan   I used to always play football and just be a bit of a lad like, you know, when I was younger. And I used to work away from home a lot. But, you know, one of my good mates I've met since, his missus, she works, she's in that side, and so she's, she's seen *Mamma Mia!* and stuff like that.

Simon   Right.

Scott   Yeah.

Alan   I never even seen *Shrek*.

Simon   No. No. No. Right.

And, and, uh, and how old are you, Alan? You're . . .?

Alan   Fifty-four.

Simon   Fifty-four? Uh, and you're from Corby?

Alan   Yeah, I was born here.

Simon   And lived here all your life? And, and you've got children?

Alan   Yeah.

Simon   How many children have you got?

Alan   I've got a daughter. She's eight.

Simon   Just the one . . .?

Alan   Yeah.

Simon   What's her name?

Alan   Lois.

Simon   So the first question, the first proper question is what's the, what's the earliest memory of your father?

Alan   Um, my, my, my father was like a really good footballer when he was younger and, um most of my time was either going with my old man to football to watch him play and, you know, meet some blokes and that, you know, you kind of get into it really and . . .

Simon   Is there one specific time you remember? One specific match or time you went with him?

Alan   Not really no.

Simon   What position did he play?

Alan   Centre midfielder.

Simon   Right.

Alan He was away all the time. I never saw him. It never bothered me. I respected it. He was working. He was in the same industry as me. He was always away in them days, you know, so . . .

Simon What industry's that?

Alan Construction. Construction. My old man spent a few years in Saudi Arabia and stuff so he lived away for quite a few years.

Simon Did you go with him or did he just go?

Alan I, I had a week out there once when I was a teenager and that was about it really.

Simon How old were you?

Alan Uh, fifteen, oh sorry sixteen. That was the first time I spent any proper time with him, like.

Simon What was that like?

Alan Brutal.

Simon In what way?

Alan It was an absolute eye-opener like, you know. That whole country.

Simon: In terms of . . .?

Alan When people go on about Muslims and immigrants and religious rights and that. The PC brigades.

When you actually go to these places, yeah? And see for your own eyes . . . the state of what they actually live in. All them Saudi Arabians, this is the one thing my dad said about them, they all think the white man is what you would say is the brains of the operation. The industrialist. They bring all the Filipinos and Indians over to that part of the world. That's slave labour like, you know, so. It will never change. It's only this country where it's like PC mental, that people get really angry and go fucking mental when you're trying to highlight what the truth of what Muslim life is actually like. It is an eye-opener. And this country, our country is going to be fucked basically, yeah. He took me to a stoning when I was there that first time.

Simon A stoning?

Alan Yeah.

Scott Fuck!

Simon You saw somebody get stoned to death?

Alan That's right.

Simon Who, who, who was stoned?

Alan Oh, I think if I remember rightly it was probably, um, a bit of adultery or something like that, back in Saudi Arabia, but nothing changes. It never shocked me. Didn't bother me. I remember thinking that I wasn't bothered.

Craig I remember falling asleep . . . on my grandad's knee at the age of two and hearing the theme tune to *Match of the Day*. It's the most comforting sort of sound. When I hear that music today, I instantly . . . They've changed the sound but I always . . . I remember we used to watch Frank Cannon together. That was on before *Match of the Day* and then I'd sit . . . You know that sort of falling asleep in your, in your, dad's arms, in my granddad's arms but *Match of the Day* was . . . It would sort of rouse me just, just enough to watch the first five minutes.

Alan Really my gran used to look after me more than anybody. My mum's mum, which was kind of weird like. She was the only one I ever knew, of all the grandparents

Craig He got paid on a Friday. Steelworks. If he went home on a Friday my nana got some money to pay the bills and what-not. If he got to the bookies first or the pub first, she wouldn't see him 'til Monday. Back to work and all the money was gone. And I don't think he could keep his dick in his pants either.

She kicked him out in the end. I think what had happened was he'd got to the house in such a state she'd had enough. I remember staying there at weekends and having candles and thinking, God, this is so exciting, you know, candlelight, but it wasn't exciting really. They just hadn't paid the electric bill.

I'd go to the local pub with him, which was the Phoenix, at the age of four. We'd sit in the corner and I'd be the only child in there. I remember people always sending drinks over. He'd never have to get out of his seat to get a, a beer because I think when it kicked off, he was, he was a bit handy.

We all hurt people sometimes, don't we?

Alan I'm quite sort of insular now 'cause, you know, my little one I've got now, right? Woe betide anyone ever touched her or done anything to her. I would quite happily spend the rest of my days in prison. I would execute anybody that touched her.

Scott Fucking hell.

Karl I know.

Scott Jesus.

Karl Fuck.

Simon He's fucking amazing. Woe betide? His exact phrasing was fucking amazing.

Scott What the fuck must he think about us eh?

What time are we getting there?

Simon Should be about an hour.

I always think it's going to be a lot more shit than it actually is.

Scott What?

Simon Stockport.

Karl And who are we seeing?

Simon A few people. A couple of people I found on Twitter.

Karl Right.

Simon Steve. My stepdad.

Steve Hello, Simon!

Scott What's he like?

Simon He's all right.

Steve Thank you, Simon.

Scott Yeah?

Simon Yeah. He's been very good to my mum.

Steve Oh. Don't get me started!

Scott Right.

Simon And then Daniel who, he's my oldest friend.

Daniel I'm not a father myself. I'm not likely to become one anytime soon.

Scott That's okay, Daniel.

Karl That's fine.

Daniel Um, I, I . . . I've been on my own for so long, um, I, I sort of . . . I just, I . . . I found it very difficult.

Scott I think everybody's different experience informs the whole piece. I don't think you need to apologise about it or worry or.

Simon No.

Scott So, Daniel, you're the seventh person that we've interviewed.

Karl And the first person we've made a cup of tea for.

Daniel Thank you.

Simon You all right?

Daniel   I'm fine. Great. Fantastic.

Simon   Um, okay so Scott's going to interview you. And I'm just going to pull faces.

Scott   So I'll just start with a first question and we'll just play from there, but we've asked everybody what's the earliest memory of your father?

Song: 'We All Hurt People Sometimes'

Karl   We're rolling now.

Daniel   The first memories are of getting upset with my dad winding me up. We'd go on a sort of day out or something, you know, with the family and we'd, we'd, you know, go to a . . . we'd be like, in the grounds of some tourist attraction place and, I'd see, I'd see the car driving off or something, you know, and, just being, being in tears thinking that, 'God they're all . . . My dad's driving off on me', and, uh . . .

I think it was the, you know, and to a, to a middle-aged man it was funny, you know, it was a good laugh. So, so, so of course the car comes back, you know. But to a, to a like a really young kid it's a bit, 'Fucking hell'.

Craig (*sings*)   My dad was married when he met my mum

Steve   I was telling your mum about this, Simon. When I was a kid I used to go for walks with my sister . . .

Craig (*sings*)   My mum's never really filled me in about the story

Steve   There's a series of canals running out of Stockport. And every Sunday we used to walk along them.

Craig (*sings*)   It's not something we really connect about

Steve   Once it was pouring with rain and my dad actually went home – we had no coats on, and we had this thunderstorm, and my dad walked all the way home and got our coats and came back with them, our coats.

Daniel   He, he was really funny and, um, affectionate with us as, as young, as young kids. Yeah, he was affectionate, you know, for, for, for like when we were knee-high kids, um, um, yeah, and he, he told stuff that made us laugh, yeah, yeah, yeah, he had us in stitches sometimes, yeah, he was funny at times, yeah.

Craig (*sings*)   I think he was twenty-three. My mum was sixteen

Steve   He was a United fan.

Craig (*sings*)   She was hanging around outside the pub, looking in

Daniel   He had a bit of a comb-over going on I think in the seventies. He had a big, big coat, you know, a big car dealer coat, you know, and things like that. A few old suits I saw were kind of thrown, you know, thrown in the cellar and they were like seventies monstrosity suits, you know. Really, really, really take your eyes out, you know. He thought he was James Bond.

Craig (*sings*)   She was seventeen . . .

All (*sing*)   Ooooo

Craig (*sings*)   by the time she had me.

All (*sing*)   Ooooo

Craig (*sings*)   He was just a young lad looking for a young girl on the go

Steve   I tell you what my dad was – he was, he was a very good pianist. He could, he could – we had one of these upright pianos, and he could play. He'd never read music in his life, and he could play the piano like Winifred Atwell.

Craig (*sings*)   I was born nine months later.
I was born nine months later.

Daniel   He still to this day watches Steven Seagal films, he finds them really interesting. Watches them again and again, you know, he loves all the action films, you know. Have you seen him? Have you seen his fighting? He just doesn't move. It's just like that. He's amazing.

Steve   He was unbelievably good.

And he also had a piano accordion, you know.

All (*sing*)   I remember falling asleep on my grandad's knee
and hearing the theme tune to *Match of the Day*.
It's the most comforting sort of sound.
I remember going to the local pub at the age of four.
We'd sit in the corner and I'd be the only child.
Never had to get out of his chair.
They'd always send over a beer.
I think when it kicked off,
he was a little bit handy.

Craig (*sings*)   We all hurt people sometimes

All (*sing*)   We all hurt people sometimes

Steve (*sings*)   We all hurt people sometimes

All (*sing*)   We all hurt people sometimes

Daniel (*sings*)   We all hurt people sometimes

All (*sing*)   We all hurt people sometimes
We all hurt people sometimes
We all hurt people sometimes
We all hurt people sometimes
We all . . .
We all . . .

Daniel   He had about three vinyl LPs. He had like Frank Sinatra, he had, uh, Glenn Miller. He was, he was a real sort of throwback in many ways with his musical taste.

I think music was an escape for me. It was, it was, it was an escape like, um, drawing and writing. Going down the rabbit hole. I would happily draw and write . . . for, for, you know, days, weeks. I'm not sure if he ever understood that.

I went to study art. Uh, fine art at, um, university. He never went to university or college or anything like that.

It . . . uh . . . it was good for a few years . . . maybe some good friends, um, but . . . uh . . . then there was a kind of an episode with, um, uh, slide into my mental ill health and sort of slide, sliding into that and that, that, that, that kind of . . . um . . . you know, that was, that was kind of the course that, that things went after that and . . . um . . . Yeah. Yeah, I . . . uh . . . I took, uh, I took a couple of years out, um, sort of, you know, try and get my, my head back together and, um, went back . . . um . . . finished the final year . . . uh . . . and came out with a 2:1 which was . . . astonishing considering I'd really, I'd really fuck, fucked . . . things up, you know, in a major way

Luke   Can I ask you? Why are you doing this?

Was that rude? I'm sorry.

Scott   No.

Luke   I didn't mean to be rude.

Simon   You weren't rude, we're just not sure what you mean by your question.

Luke   Why are you doing these interviews? What are you hoping to achieve? Sorry. I'm being a right dick.

Simon   No, you're not. Not at all.

Scott   Do you know the film *Cloudy with a Chance of Meatballs*?

Luke   Yeah, I think so. I think I saw that with my niece.

Scott   So, so there's, there's, there's a machine in this film.

Luke   Right

Scott   'Cause it's about an inventor.

Luke   That's right. Yeah, yeah. I remember!

Scott   And he, the, er, the inventor, invents a machine which is called the Monkey Thought Translator.

Which, which is . . . He's got this pet monkey. And he invents this machine so he can hear what the monkey is thinking. But it's not much use because the monkey only ever thinks really simple things. Like 'food!' and 'Steve!' Steve's the name of his owner, the inventor.

Luke (*impersonates the monkey*)   'Steve!'

Scott   Ha! Yeah! But at the end, at the end of the film Steve has saved the whole town basically and been like a real hero and his dad is trying to tell him how he feels and he can't find the words.

Luke   Classic!

Scott   Yeah. But at the end of the film his girlfriend it is, actually, takes the machine and puts it on his dad.

Luke   That's right.

Scott   So for the first time he hears what his dad's thinking and what his dad's thinking is that he's really . . .

Simon   He's thinking what he can't say. What he's not able to say. In an attempt to bridge the communication gap between . . .

Luke   If only you knew. Kind of thing.

Simon   Yeah, if only you knew.

Scott   There's a lot I'd like to know. I wanted to put that thought translator on my father. And, and, and allow other people to er do the same.

Luke   Amazing where you can get your inspiration from, isn't it?

From Disney characters.

Simon   Exactly, yeah.

Luke   Mary Poppins next.

Simon   Ha.

Luke   So, do you all live in London, aye?

Scott   That's right.

Simon (*to* **Karl**)   Yeah, well, you're not London, are you?

Karl   Sorry, what?

Simon   You don't live in London do you?

Karl   No, I'm not in London.

Scott   I live in Surrey but I work in London a lot of the time.

Luke   I quite like London. We've been down a few times. I don't know if I'd like to live there though.

Simon   No?

Luke   Bit noisy isn't it? Compared to round here?

Karl   I like the noise. I always find the noises in cities are energising.

Luke   But you can still make a show about Kidderminster or Corby or Stockport or whatever even if you've not lived there in, how long was it?

Simon   Twenty-seven years.

Luke   Oooft.

Simon   Yeah. You can. I still think about Stockport all the time. When you get older you can kind of forgive a place. Sorry. That makes me sound like a dick. I write about Stockport, all the time.

Luke   Brilliant. Yeah. And then when you've done the interviews are you just going to go?

Alan   This is probably quite relevant, right?

When I was younger I was fairly handy. And when I got older I done a bit of boxing training and stuff like that, yeah?

Now down here, they have this village thing where they have this bus, on bank holiday weekend, and it goes round all the pubs and all the villages, right? And all the kids, all the young lads they pile on this bus and its basically like a pub crawl round the village on a bus.

And one time right there was a load of aggravation in the street and I was in the car with Lois and my missus and the aggro meant the car had got stopped and the bus was behind us and we couldn't move. And this guy, one of the boys from the bus, he reckoned we were stopping the traffic and he got off the bus and put his, this guy stuck his head into the window of my car when Lois was like, she was probably about four at the time, and this boy started giving it the large one to my missus. Lois burst into tears, I went ballistic. I nearly killed this guy. I dragged him out into the middle of the road and beat him up and his mates went nuts so I broke their fucking heads up for them and all and it was only 'cause two taxi drivers saw, jumped in, seen me and pulled me away from them . . . I just weren't having it.

And like, do you remember Graham Young? Guy goes to school?

Yeah, well I get on well with Youngie. Youngie seen that, right? But he didn't see what went off before and he, he kind of had a go at me in the pub the next, like the next day after being quizzed by the cops and that and I went, 'Youngie, you wait until you have a kid'. He's got a kid now, Hamish.

Simon   What's your dad called?

Karl   Graham.

Scott   Where are we meeting him?

Karl   At his house. In Bewdley. And then actually Mel, who's one of my oldest friends he only lives next door so we'll go round to his.

Mel   Hello, Karl, mate.

Karl   He was a fireman.

Mel   That's right.

Karl   And his dad was a fireman too.

Mel   Aye.

Scott   Will your mum be at home?

Karl   She might be. Lurking.

Scott   Is this going to be very strange for you?

Karl   Just a bit.

Simon   What's he like?

Karl   He's just. He's Dad. He's –

Graham   I'm eighty-one.

Simon   Eighty-one?

Graham   Yeah, this is my eighty-second year.

Simon   Brilliant. When's your birthday, Graham?

Graham   July.

Simon   Which means you were born in 1935?

Graham   4.

Simon   Thank you.

Graham   That's all right.

Simon   And you're from Bewdley?

Graham   Yeah, born and bred.

Simon   And have lived here all your life?

Graham   All my life.

Simon   Where was your father from?

Graham Bewdley.

Simon And his father as well? Is this a town that the family's been in . . .

Graham Yes

Simon What's the earliest memory that you have of your father?

Graham Of my father?

Simon Yeah.

Graham That's the sort of question I wouldn't like to answer, actually, if you don't mind.

Simon No. Of course not. Right. Right. Right. Right.

A pause.

Song: 'Nothing Getting Built Now'

Karl (*sings*) There's nothing getting built now. Nothing, not now.

Mel So all of a sudden Kidderminster was this town that existed for no reason.

Karl (*sings*) It's just a satellite town, isn't it, I mean, I mean, it's
Somewhere on the periphery of somewhere that's pretty interesting.

Steve I like to see the positive. The houses are lovely. And you get a garden. And the prices, in comparison to –

Karl (*sings*) You can get into a big city pretty easily from here.
You can go to concerts, you can go to the cinemas,

Daniel (*sings*) you can go to pubs,
you can go to art galleries,
you can access a lot, a lot, a lot, a lot, a lot,
if you're within reach of a hub like that.

Mel   Am I optimistic about the human race? No. I think we are on a crash course. The politicians and the banks. And this referendum. What an opportunity to kick Westminster in the bollocks.

Alan (*sings*)   I think a lot of the industry was decimated,

Graham (*sings*)   like the carpet industry kind of went with all the other industries.

Graham   I will say that both my mother and father were alcoholics.

Simon   Right.

Graham   Up to the age of fourteen home life was no home life.

Simon   Right.

Graham   No.

Mum worked in a pub where she drank. Father went to a pub where he drank.

Simon   What did he do? Your dad? What was his job?

Mel   He was quite old fashioned. He was a retained firefighter, fire . . . fireman in Bewdley.

Which means basically erm we had fucking great big bell in our house.

Alan   He built roads. He built bridges.

Steve   He worked for a company called BRS. He used to drive three-wheeled trucks around Piccadilly Station. Just literally three-wheeled. Do you remember these things, Simon?

Craig   I do sometimes wonder what job he did. And when you don't know. Like if he was, I don't know. If he was a taxi driver or a builder or something what would I have been then? And when you don't know the answer to that question.

Daniel   He was working in the car trade. He'd come back with a different car every, every week or so or every other week.

He had things like Jensen Interceptors. Aston Martins. Um, Bentleys, you know, it was . . . I, I, I loved seeing a different car on the drive every couple of weeks and, and, and, and I remember once he had a beach buggy in the middle of Stockport.

Graham   They never were in love with each other, never. There you go.

I didn't see much of them until the war was over.

I couldn't comprehend what was going on. I used to sit outside at night and watch Birmingham get bombed. I couldn't say in my mind, oh, people are getting killed. To me it wasn't war. It was bonfire night.

The house I lived in was . . . It was frightening. it was never a home. If you could imagine the worst picture you've had of slums on the television, it was that bad. I mean the wallpaper just hung on the walls. We only had one gaslight in the living room. That was all. Three bedrooms, two of which we used and if the gas went, there was no one to give me money to put into the meter, so I sat outside on the bank. It was better to sit outside the house than inside the house for me.

If there was enough in the gas, then I'd stop in the house and fall asleep downstairs. I wouldn't go upstairs because it was too dark.

I do get nightmares about the house. In my mind I can walk into that house now and touch everything that's in there and tell you exactly where it was, even the marks on the ceiling that I used to look at and made pictures out of.

Luke   Why don't you just make it up?

Simon   We could. I mean we could. I mean in a way that's our job. But there's a kind of truthful quality when instead of inventing something you use the actual words that people say to you in interview.

Luke   How many interviews are you doing?

Simon   About fifteen I think.

Scott   Twelve.

Luke   Isn't it going to be a bit long?

Simon   Well we'll edit it.

Luke   What? Change things?

Simon   Not change them no.

Scott   We're not going to lie.

Luke   But if you don't include everything you're changing things aren't you? Why don't you include everything?

Simon   Because, yes, I mean, then it would be too long then.

Scott   It would go on for days!

Simon   And be really boring.

Luke   Are you worried we're all going to be really boring?

Simon   No. No. No. Not at all.

Luke   What's the difference between changing something and lying?

Simon   We're not making anything up.

Luke   But, right, the people coming to see the show, they're going to think this is what we actually said. But it's not.

Simon   Well –

Scott   I think that's a fair point.

Simon   Do you?

Scott   It's something I've thought about.

Simon   I don't think audiences are that naïve.

Luke   How do you know which bits to keep in?

Simon   I think thematically.

Luke   What do you mean?

Simon   I think we'll decide how we want the show to affect people and edit the material around that decision.

Scott   Musically.

Luke   The bits that sound good?

Karl   And the things that connect people.

Luke   Do you think we're all connected to each other?

Karl   Yes I do.

Luke   Do you?

Karl   The more places I go to, the more people I meet, the more I realise that just at those times when people think they're dislocated from one another they're more connected than they ever realise.

Luke   Bit vague, yeah? What kind of 'things' connect people?

Simon   All kinds of things.

Scott   Their first memories. Their favourite food. The music they like. Where they were born. The work they did. The way they die.

This launches into 'Melting Man'.

Song: 'Melting Man'

Mel   I've only ever been to one job where I just wanted to turn around and walk away.

So you get this piece of paper that tells you what fire engines
to send and the address and . . . the nature of the incident
and whether it's a fire or a car crash or whatever. Erm and
all these things, all this turn-out sheet said was erm proceed
to such and such address at the request of the police. (*Intro
begins.*) No blue lights. Contact control. So I thought well
that's a bit odd. So I phoned them up, phoned control up.

(*Sings.*)   And what it was, it was Christmas Eve, and these
    two lads had been round to see their dad.
    They hadn't visited for a while. Erm, knocked on the door,
    couldn't make anybody hear. Shouted through the
    letterbox.
    'Dad! Dad!'
    the stink was . . . incredible.
    So they called the police,
    And he'd been dead for about six weeks.

So we pulled up to this address and the coppers came out to
meet us with an undertaker who'd arrived by then. And the
copper his . . . his face was as white as his shirt.

(*Sings.*)   And this old undertaker
    looked green
    this guy when he'd fallen asleep, he'd had one of these
    portable gas heaters on. Full pelt. He'd melted into the
    bedclothes. And up the wall.

Like damp.

(*Sings.*)   You could see the mark where he was . . . he was
    . . . the fluid from him was going up the wall,

like damp. I don't know if they told his sons. They'd not
been to see him for weeks, like.

The undertakers had put him in a . . . in a casket. But this
was er like a two-up two . . . two-down house. They couldn't
carry him out level. Every time they tipped the casket up he
leaked out of it all over the shop. And they were just at their
wits' end as to what to do with him.

(*Sings.*)   So the thing with the fire service is
   we're the last . . . sometimes in a job like that the last
   people that they call . . . and if we can't do it there's
   nobody else.
   So we've got to do it.
   I thought, I don't want to do this job, I wanna go home.
   We wrapped the casket in plastic bags that you use in the
   event of chemical contamination,
   we put them round the . . . round the round the coffin,
   tied it up. Even if it did leak it was all contained in these
   plastic bags.

All his organs had melted and everything. Most of it was in
his bedclothes.

(*Sings.*)   And up the wall!

Like damp. We were getting dust masks and filling them. We
found a tube of germolene in the bathroom, and we started
filling the dust masks with germolene to get rid of the smell.
And that would last about five minutes and then the smell
would come through again. And in the end we'd run out of
germolene and we was using linseed oil putty in these . . . in
these dust masks. So every time I smell linseed oil putty now
I think of that . . . poor old bloke who melted. And his sons,
like. Go and see Dad at Christmas.

'Dad! Dad!'

Alan   He had a, you know, a bad brain tumour, you know, it
went on and on and on for ever, you know. And one of the
effects of the tumour was that it stopped him keeping his
mouth shut. Whatever he thought he just said it.

It was like hilarious at first, like you know when you're in
hospital? And he's like, 'Oh don't let that big fat nurse near
me', but he was actually saying it, and then the little Thai
one would come and he'd go, 'Why can't you come and bed
bath me? I used to do birds like you when I was in Saudi.'

Simon   Ha!

Daniel   He did find my illness difficult. I think he found the idea of mental illness difficult on the whole. Um, I don't know if it would have been different if I'd broken my arm or like had cancer or something, I, I, I've never asked him about that but maybe I will, maybe I will ask him about that.

Alan   He could say what he wanted to say . . .

Simon   He had the Monkey Thought Translator!

Scott   Yeah.

Alan   Funny enough yeah, my missus, she always goes on about this. He was in his wheelchair. I went to push the buttons to stop it moving but the buttons didn't work and it just kept going, and my old man went, 'Fucking typical, what a fucking cunt. Just let your old man smash into the fucking wall you fucking wanker.' That was his exact words. My missus was killing herself like, yeah. So there you go. That's what he thinks about me.

Luke   Are you going to change our names? Are you going to tell everybody you're interviewing how you're going to use all our answers and how you might change them and things like that? Sorry? Am I being a bit of a twat?

Scott   No.

Luke   I feel like I'm being a bit of a twat.

Scott   You're not being a twat.

Simon   But we do need to get back to the interview.

Luke   How much money are you going to make out of this show?

Simon   I don't think it's possible to tell really. Not at this stage?

Luke   How much money do you normally make?

Simon   What?

Luke   Last year how much money did you make last year? More than me probably eh?

Simon   Hm.

Luke   I made twenty-three grand. Did you make more than that?

Simon   Daniel. Can I ask you? Did your dad ever tell you he loved you?

Song: 'Not a Word' (a cappella version – **Daniel** *attempts this but has to stop)*

Daniel (*sings*)   No. We don't say the word love . . .
   No we don't say the word . . . to any . . .
   to each other but we kind of try
   and do the best we can for each other I guess.

Karl   Fuck. Shit.

Scott   Sorry.

Karl   I swear I turned it off.

Daniel   It was just the right moment . . . I was about to break down!

Simon   Please . . .

Steve   I mean, the, the, the thing we laughed about was he used to smoke. I tried to get him to stop but he wouldn't. My mum stopped him smoking in the house, and he used to go down the bottom of the garden – my mum's got this, got this wooden gate at the bottom, and he used to sit – he used to go and smoke at the bottom of the garden, like this, with his elbows on the gate, and he got an infection through his elbows off the wood, because, you know from the – cracks on the elbows, he got an infection through his elbows. So he did have to stop for a bit.

Simon   Do you need a break or anything?

Mel   We get a phone call to say he's been taken ill and
they've called an ambulance. We go straight to the hospital
which had an A&E department then and we pulled up just
erm . . . just as he . . . as the ambulance pulled in to the A&E.
And they opened the back doors and he's in there. And I
knew, cos I was a fireman by then so I knew these things. Er
I knew straightaway from the equipment they'd got on him
that it was bad. Erm he'd got an airway in and stuff like that.
I thought oh this isn't good. And within twenty minutes he
was dead. He was forty-six.

Simon   Is there anything I can get you?

Steve   My brother was getting married, the youngest
brother and my dad was really ill, ah, and then, ah, we
thought he was doing quite well and then he, on Boxing Day
– we always used to have, um – my mum always used to do a,
a, family party, get-together on Boxing Day, and, ah, he
collapsed on Boxing Day at about 7 o'clock. He went to the
toilet and I had to smash the door down to get in, um, and
cleaned him up – he was in a right mess. Anyway, they took
him into hospital and he died the next day, next morning.
And I, I was – I'm going to get upset now, because I stayed
with Mum all night with him, and at 8 o'clock in the
morning, um, I said, 'I'm going to go home and get changed
and come back'. And I'd been gone for twenty minutes, and
I got a phone call saying he'd died after I'd gone. So I was
upset about that. But, you know.

Graham   He had a heart attack, I think because of the drink.

Craig   I said my piece to him when he was lying there . . . I
just told him that I loved him, you know, you know, and I'll
see you soon, one day, grandad. I mean, it wasn't anything
poetic or great, just that I loved him and what I thought
about him and I remember him sort of squeezing my hand
sort of a bit.

Song: 'Not a Word'

Mel It was a erm full fire-brigade funeral . . . with a fire engine . . . and everything. Like all the uniforms and everything. And like I say I was a fireman by then as well.

I got to a higher rank than my dad did. I trained the kids of people that he'd worked with. I trained their sons. I reckon that his chest would have been out here at that sort of thing.

He died on 21 December so really fucked up our Christmas yeah. Yeah because 21 December now we always, we go to the grave and we put flowers on and erm . . . and wreaths or some. It's like the start of Christmas now. We'd get to the grave and then we . . . we usually go to a pub on the way back and have a meal and . . .

I dream about him. He's just there. It is just a presence.

Daniel (*sings*) No we don't say the word love . . .
No we don't say the word . . . to any . . .
To each other but we kind of try
and do the best we can for each other I guess.

No . . . it's a word . . . um . . . we don't really . . . Um . . .
just the right moment there. When I was about to break down.
Uh . . . it's a word . . . we don't really use . . .
um . . . in . . . in . . . family encounters.

No it's not a word . . . we don't really . . . Um

No it's not a word . . .

No it's not a word . . .

No it's not a word . . .

Luke What's it like coming home?

Scott It's good. It's odd. It's odd seeing the place I grew up in with these two because they're seeing it for the first time and so it's like I end up seeing it for the first time too.

Luke Do you still think of this as being your home?

Scott   Yes.

It just is. It always will be. I can't change that. The place you grow up makes you who you are even if you don't like it.

Luke   Then why did you leave?

Scott   What?

Luke   Why did you leave if this is your home?

Karl   Just because you think of a place as being your home doesn't mean you have to like it.

Luke   No?

Karl   No.

Luke   No.

Karl   When I was growing up my hometown made me feel like a freak because of the way I looked at the world. It was sucking the life out of me. Why the fuck would you hang around in a place like that?

Luke   Right. (*To* **Scott**.) Has it changed much?

Scott   I don't know if Corby's changed or I just see it differently now.

Luke   Why do you see it differently?

Scott   I'm older. I see things for the first time that I've not noticed before.

Luke   What kind of things.

Scott   The physical geography. How the roads fit together.

Luke   The 'physical geography'?

Karl   Yeah. The shape of the land. The weather. The proximity to water. You move around as much as we do and you start to notice that these things change places.

Luke   Is that right?

Karl Yes it is.

Luke Course. What about you?

Simon Me?

Luke Yeah. You. What's it going to be like for you going back to your hometown?

Song: 'Perfect Moment'

Simon Where were you when you found out you were going to become a father?

Craig (*sings*) My grandad had just died.
  We went up to see the grave and visit him.
  And we were together
  and you're gonna think this is the perfect moment to tell me.
  So, we're together, chatting about things and life and death and my grandad.
  And the sun was shining.

Luke No. Come on, man.

Simon Come on, man, what?

Luke Answer my question. What's it going to be like for you going back to Stockport?

Simon Can I ask you, how did you feel? Do you remember?

Craig (*sings*) We went home and she never said a word
  then we were arguing ten minutes later and she went 'Oh I'm pregnant'.
  And I was really gutted.
  I said, 'Why didn't you tell me ten minutes ago at the graveside?' Spielberg could have directed it. I even had a tear rolling down my eye.
  For my grandad.
  She says, 'Don't worry. You're having a little girl.'

Song: 'No Feeling Like This'

Craig (*sings*)   When she was born I remember
picking her up and any drug that I'd taken,
I wouldn't.

If my kids did drugs I'd be heartbroken
and I'm gonna try and take them to where they don't do
drugs.
But I had some Dennis the Menace in my time.

Have been fantastic!
Have been fantastic!

Had great nights on drugs and enjoyed them totally
but I remember at this point thinking there isn't any
feeling in the world to beat, you know, when you break,
you just start sobbing, don't you!

Have been fantastic!

You've got your girl in your hands.
There wasn't a feeling like it. And I went home and it
didn't wear off,
you know, the, the, the, the, the feeling, feeling, feeling
Unlike with drugs, you didn't have a come-down. It went
on that day.
I went to bed that night. She stayed in.

Have been fantastic!
Have been fantastic!
Have been fantastic!
Fantastic!
Fantastic!

Luke   Is there a reason you don't want to answer that
question?

Simon   Where were you when you found out you were
going to become a father?

Steve   I was here.

Simon   In Stockport?

Steve   That's right. We were engaged for a while and then she got, she got pregnant. I wanted to do things properly so we got married.

Luke   You're not avoiding it are you?

Simon   Where were you when you found out you were going to become a father?

Alan   I was in the boozer. It was like, 'Oh man, mad!' do you know what I mean? It's like it is a hard thing to explain. It's like when you see the first, you know, you go for scans and all that.

I've always said this to people, right? And this is the one thing I always say, right? When my missus gave birth, right? She went through like torture, yeah? Everything you could name was wrong like and it was like the, the film . . . It was like a film, film set when you seen the amount of blood she had . . . It was like that film *Hostel*, it was like a slaughter scene everywhere.

Luke   It's not even a very personal question. Is it?

Simon   Where were you when you found out you were going to become a father?

Mel   I was on a fire that week, cos she was a week late and the day which she was supposed to arrive I was actually on a big fire in Kidderminster. And erm and Hereford and Worcester Fire Brigade/Fire Control was on alert that if they got a phone call they'd contact me on the radio on the fire engine and I'd be off.

Luke   What was it you were looking for when you went back home? Is that what you meant when you talked about forgiveness?

Simon   Where were you when you found out you were going to become a father?

Graham   I was on RNVR service. I was down in Portsmouth on board a ship for a fortnight. Royal Navy Volunteer Reserve. It was awful really. I received a letter saying, and the phrase was 'we've got a child on the way'. I mean, we were all sat round the mess table reading our mail and all of a sudden I said 'I'm going to be a dad' and there was a silence. I thought, well, come on . . . I would have much rather she waited until I got home so I could go 'yippee, hoo, haw'. All I wanted to do was hug her and say 'wow, magic' and all that sort of business. Whether she felt that way, I don't know.

Karl was not a pretty child.

Karl   Right. Thanks, Dad. Nice one.

Graham   We'd go out for a walk and people would say 'Oh, can we look at the baby' and if he was awake, she'd have him covered up and say 'Don't wake him, he's asleep' because he was ugly. Did you ever see or read Dan Dare comics?

Well, there was a character in there who was Dan Dare's enemy. He was the Mekon.

Karl had a head like the Mekon.

Song: 'This Is My Son'

Graham   When I first met Karl, that very first time, I wanted the reaction where I'm giving everybody cigars, but I didn't get it.

Graham (*sings*)   I've only ever told one person about this.
    Even Sandra doesn't know because we
    agreed that Sandra would take care of the top end, and I
    would take care of the bottom end.

    She would feed, I would dispose and he was always, he
    wakes up in the night time.
    Better see what he wants.
    Phew! Nappy!
    You didn't have disposable nappies,
    we had terry towelling nappies, wipes.
    And I didn't put, I hadn't put on, I hadn't put on one
    before.
    I put the pin in, picked him up and it dropped off.

I thought that's no good.
So I put it on again.
And previously I had seen him and I wanted the reaction
where I am giving everybody cigars but I had no reaction.
I thought 'Oh, that's my son'. But when I picked him up
that second time, we looked at each other, at one another
. . .
I've got to stop.

And then there was no one around, just him and me, and
no one. The whole place lit up.
It was alight.
It was great and now I just wanted it to go on to go out in
the street and shout 'This is my son'!

And was no one there, just him and me and no one.
The whole place lit up.
And I was alight.
It was great and now I just wanted it to go on I just
wanted to go out in the street and shout 'This is my son'!

This is my son!
This is my son!
This is my son!
This is my son!

This. Is. My. Son!
This. Is. My. Son!
This. Is. My. Son!
This. Is. My. Son!
This. Is. My. Son!

The next morning I got up . . . I got up before he shouted
and I picked him up and looked and I didn't get no reaction
at all, none at all, but I'd had that reaction, that wonderful
reaction. And that didn't happen again until Karl received a
prize from school. I think he's still got it. It's a dictionary the
mayor gave to him, and it happened again. No one there.
The school was full, but there was no one there, me and him.
Yeah, and it's my whole body tingled, as if I'd been plugged

into the mains, and it still happens now when I see him on stage.

Luke   Do you think this is going to be in any way interesting to anybody apart from you?

Simon   I think it definitely will be.

Scott   I think people are always interested in how people live.

Steve   When I was thirty-three my wife said to me she wanted to come off the pill so would I mind having a vasectomy? So I said, 'Well, yeah, that's all right'. So I had a vasectomy. Then she said to me, 'I've decided, I think it's better if I put all the money from the catering into a separate bank account in my name'. 'Oh, that's all right – no problem.' And then she decided that she wanted to do this trip, a Rhine and wine trip. And she came back at the end of October in '85, and she said to me, 'I'm going in four weeks'. So I just said, I just said, 'Are you going on another holiday?' And she says, 'No, I'm leaving'. So I said, 'Leaving where?' She said, 'I don't want to be married anymore'.

She went on 1 December, and it was our Colin's birthday on 10 December, and she moved out and left me with the kids, two teenage girls and a little boy, and I raised them from then on my own. I was a single father with three kids. I got them through school, their exams, their, their, their periods and all that. This was in the eighties. Before it was, you know, fashionable.

Luke   Are you going to put that in the show?

Alan   We, we play football. Me and Lois. I was trying to explain to her the other day about how, how come Lionel Messi was so good, yeah?

'How comes you like Messi?' You'd be like well "cause he's just got it in him'. You just can't explain it.

She turns to me, she says to me, 'I bet you were as good as Messi, Dad?' I'm like?! The idea that she might like me that much. That she might think I could be that good!

Luke What about that bit?

Luke Is that what this is for you, do you think? Living in London and finding out how other people live in different parts of the country?

Simon I think it's one of the things.

Song: 'To the Pub'

Luke (*sings*) There's a lot I'd like to know, a lot I'd like
  to know
  A lot I'd like to know, a lot I'd like to know

Graham I wanted to make it different. I wanted to show the world that it could be different. Having been brought up in that manner. I should have been impregnated with all that horribleness. I didn't want my children to ever have that. It's still there, even now it's still there.

Daniel (*sings*) I go to the pub with him.
  I go to the club with him.
  I have a pint, watch a match

Graham I can see every minute of it . . . The thought of living in that house.

Daniel (*sings*) but . . . he still disappoints me a lot . . .
  but . . . you know but I'm not gonna slag him off.
  Y'know, it's just who he is

Graham I can go through most of the arguments they ever had.

Daniel (*sings*) You got to kind of, you got to have some sort
  of acceptance of who people are.
  You know, even when you, you really can't bring yourself
  to like them all the time, you know.

Graham   I shut them out and they go away. They don't bother me now. They don't bother me. I have bad dreams about the house . . . Sounds, the deathwatch beetle in the wood.

Daniel (*sings*)   If I could ask him anything.
   If I could really hear what he was thinking.
   There'd, there'd be a lot that I'd like to know.

All (*sing*)   There's a lot I'd like to know, a lot I'd like to know.
   A lot I'd like to know, a lot I'd like to know.
   A lot I'd like to know, a lot I'd like to know.
   A lot I'd like to know, a lot I'd like to know.

Daniel (*sings*)   You've done all this for, the three of us,
   y' know, you've worked so hard,
   but at the same time you've, you've you know,
   you've really given us a lot of grief,
   and and it's been a bloody rollercoaster.
   It's been, it's been a massive but well massive, massive trauma.

   Family life has been really tough,
   but you, you know you stayed.
   What, was it that you were putting all of that devotion and energy and commitment, into,
   was it worth it,
   you know it is is it, worth that,
   you know, do you feel that it's, um,
   is it what you were, is it what you were doing it for?

Luke (*sings*)   There's a lot I'd like to know, a lot I'd like to know.
   A lot I'd like to know, a lot I'd like to know.

All (*sing*)   A lot I'd like to know, a lot I'd like to know.
   A lot I'd like to know, a lot I'd like to know.
   A lot I'd like to know, a lot I'd like to know.
   A lot I'd like to know, a lot I'd like to know.

A lot I'd like to know, a lot I'd like to know.
A lot I'd like to know, a lot I'd like to know.

Chorus Only (*sing*)   A lot I'd like to know, a lot I'd like
to know.
A lot I'd like to know, a lot I'd like to know.
A lot I'd like to know, a lot I'd like to know.
A lot I'd like to know, a lot I'd like to know.

Luke   Are you going to interview yourselves?

Simon   We already have done.

Luke   Are you going to use those interviews?

Simon   No. That wasn't the point of them. It was how we
tested out the process and the questions and what worked
and what didn't.

Luke   If you did use them would you play yourselves.

Simon   I doubt that very much.

Scott   We'd get actors to play us.

Karl   We're not going to use our interviews.

Luke   Why not?

Karl   Because it's not a show about us.

Luke   Isn't it?

Simon   It would feel self-indulgent.

Luke   Isn't all your work self-indulgent?

Simon   What?

Karl   Sorry?

Scott   What?

Luke   What was the earliest memory you have of your
father?

Simon   I thought you said you'd never seen any of my plays.

Luke   What's the earliest memory you have of your father?

What's the earliest memory you have of your father?

Alan   What's the earliest memory you have of your father?

Steve   What's the earliest memory you have of your father?

Graham   What's the earliest memory you have of your father?

Karl   He built me um uh like a covered wagon. Um and from you know some . . . from the Wild West and pulled me around hidden in that

Scott   The anticipation of waiting for him to come home on a Saturday afternoon because he'd work Saturday mornings and come home and have a quick snack, then he'd take me off to the football and that felt so exciting, you know, waiting.

Whenever we scored, which wasn't that often, I'd find him turn around to me and throwing me up in the air and, and embracing, uh, me, um, and, you know. I think there was an incredible thrill to have your little boy and, and kind of throw him in the air.

Karl   Travelling in his car. I liked that a lot because we listened to the radio a lot. From a very early age the car was a film. You know car . . . the windscreen was a film screen.

And the . . . and the radio was the set . . . was the score. And it always has been.

Scott   He ruled his house. He earned the money. I remember the way he sat. He felt he had the right to be that person who sits on the sofa while things happen around him,

He seemed to live in quite a cruel world.

When he comes over, but when they come over to spend time with my kids, he sits reading the newspaper, and, and I am just like, 'Why aren't you grabbing every fucking moment you can with these kids? Why aren't you tickling them? Why aren't you throwing them up in the air?' I said this to my brother and he says, 'Well why would they? They never did it with us.'

Karl Of course you never had seat belts in them days.

And uh we were coming back from the picnic a beautiful day. I don't know. I think I fell asleep. I woke up and the car was upside down.

And as it happens I was launching through the windscreen and my dad put his arm out and knocked me back over the bench seat. He stopped me.

And the only people that weren't hurt was my dad, me and my mum. The kid next to me shot through the windscreen and ended up on the road the other side And . . . and I . . . I came to on my mum's lap absolutely gutted that my little plastic boat was out in the middle of the road and kind of scattered all over the . . . All our picnic was all over the floor but I . . . I . . . I had just had this little plastic fishing boat was on the . . . it was red, blue and yellow, primary colours and uh . . . and um I was just you know, just in bits because my boat was in the middle of the road and it just felt there's this huge invasion of this personal cocoon space that I'd grown up in. It was just ripped to shreds.

Simon I remember we went to Blackpool for a day trip, and I remember looking up at what to my head looked like an enormous stallion, and looking at my dad on top of this huge horse, but he was never a horse rider, so it can't have been a horse, because to ride a proper horse you need a certain amount of experience and skill.

It must have been a Blackpool donkey, but in my head it was like I was looking up at this tower of a man astride a horse.

This is a dreadful confession I'm about to make, and this will change everything and might actually end the project, but my dad raised me a Manchester City fan. I used to go to Maine Road with him and watch football with him at Maine Road and watch football on the telly with him. And there's a big long story about how I fell out of love with football and out of love with Man City, and how Eric Cantona, when he came to Man United, got me back into it. It was actually one of my wedding vows. My wife vowed never to tell anybody.

My dirty secret. It is quite . . .

It's as dirty as you can get.

I've always had this thing about father figures. And I think Cantona was, he was. I have no idea what my dad thought about it. We laughed about it but I do wonder if he felt betrayed.

But then, you know, the last Christmas present before he died, though, this was when he was fifty-seven, I think. Maybe fifty-eight. He must have known he was dying. He was meant to stop drinking and he didn't even though he knew that if he didn't he would die. And at this time he was working as a door-to-door salesman. Selling fucking *Manchester Evening News* subscriptions in the shittiest parts of Stockport you can imagine. The last Christmas present he got me he gave me was a Cantona shirt. Number 7 on the back.

Luke   Is that you's done? Come on, guys? We're just getting started here.

Song: 'It Isn't Me'

Simon   And now I'm turning into him. I used to spend far too long in the toilet. He would get really impatient. I don't know what I did in there that took so long, and it used to take me a long time to get my shoes on and he used to get furious.

And now I find myself getting impatient, in the way that my dad did with me, about things like – 'How long do you need to be on the fucking toilet for? You know, we've got to go!' 'Get your shoes on – it's school! For God's sake, come on!' 'Put your fucking shoes on!' I'm exactly the same as he was.

Karl (*sings*)   My room was above the kitchen.
I could hear the sounds coming through the floor . . .
crashing pots and pans and my mum would start singing
these kind of mad songs . . .
She was singing but it was in like, like she was saying
'I'm going to kill everybody'
'I'm going to kill everybody'
'I'm going to kill everybody'
'I'm going to kill everybody'
And eventually Dad would get in the car and drive off . . .

And you could hear his car . . . for miles.

As a kid when we bought a new dustbin
I'd go sit in it and just peer at the world . . .

I'd go sit in it there and look at the world
out of this tiny slit thinking they can't see me.
They can't see me, but I can see them.
But they can't see me but I can see them but they can't see
me!

Years later as a drunk, as a drunk, I would walk around
the streets of Soho looking out, looking out through these
pinholes going, going, going, going
you can't fucking see me . . .
you can't fucking see me.
you can't fucking see me.
you can't fucking see me.

Scott (*sings*)   My brother was already there, as I walked
through the hospital,
I just seen my mum.
And my mum sees me. She just looks away.
And my brother's like, okay, and comes walking towards
me. And I think, he's fucking dead, he's dead, he's dead,
he's fucking dead, He's fucking dead.
And when I get there, I realise he's not.

And then they say, look, we're gonna transfer him to a
specialist unit,

thirty miles away, and the nurse says, it's this time in the
ambulance that's gonna be the most dangerous.
And, there is a chance that he won't make it, and, you
should come and say somethin' – goodbye, or whatever
. . .
And so they wheel him in . . .
I don't know what to do!
Then my brother takes one pace in front of me . . .
He hugs and kisses dad.
I never would have done that . . . if I'd a gone first.
I wouldn't have done that!
I wouldn't have done that!
I wouldn't have done that!
I wouldn't have done that!
I wouldn't have done that!
I wouldn't have done that!
I wouldn't have done that!
I wouldn't have done that!

Simon (*sings*)   He was raised in a culture in the seventies
and eighties
where a successful salesman would be the person who
would charm you over dinner.
So alcohol became part of his modus operandi.
And all of a sudden it's not lunch and dinner –
it's breakfast meetings and it's coffee and it's mineral
water,
he went from being somebody who drank to being an
alcoholic.
Within ten years, he was unemployed!
At the end of his life, he would go out every morning.
he'd have the paper
he'd have his flat cap,
and I'd look down
into his pockets
and there'd be a full can of cheap cider . . . at 11a.m. in
the morning.

And I don't think that I would ever have written the plays
that I've written
if that didn't happen!

I wouldn't be doing this, if it wasn't for that!
I wouldn't be doing this, if it wasn't for that
I wouldn't be doing this, if it wasn't for that
I wouldn't be doing this, if it wasn't for that

Some time.

When you say you're not going to do it?

Luke   I've been thinking about it.

Simon   Right.

Luke   And I've decided that it's not a thing that I want to be
part of.

Scott   You said said you were interested in being involved.

Luke   That was before I knew what you were asking me
to do.

Scott   Right. Well. Right. Well. That's.

Simon   That's disappointing.

Luke   I think you're lying to people.

Simon   Lying's a bit strong.

Scott   Thanks, er, thanks for that, Luke.

Luke   I think you're lying to people about why you're
interested in their stories and what you're going to do
with them.

Scott   We're not lying.

Karl   I should probably get the er, the microphone.

Luke   I think you're trying to make money out of other
people's lives.

Simon   It's not about the money.

Karl   Can I just. Just take the lead.

Luke   I think you're looking at the whole rest of this country from where you live and you're probably worried because you feel a bit guilty about how much money there is in London and how much money there is everywhere else and that kind of thing wouldn't worry bankers and that or accountants or politicians but for artists it must be a bit odd and you're going on a little daytrip to get ideas and make it seem like you really care about what life is like here for people like me or people like my dad or his dad or my mum or my sister or anybody and you don't. You just don't.

And you call it something like *Fatherland*. Do you know what the people I work with think about when they hear those words in this country now? Have you even thought about that?

So. I'm. I'm.

Karl   Thanks.

Luke   I'm just going to . . .

Scott   Right.

Simon   Have you got far to go?

Luke   No I'm just going back home. Might go to the gym.

Simon   Good idea.

Luke   What time's your next interview?

Scott   Half an hour.

Luke   Magic.

Scott   This is you.

Simon   You've got everything?

Luke   Yes. Yes. Yes. Yes.

Simon   Got your coat?

Luke   Thank you.

Simon   For example.

Luke   Maybe it's not that I think that you're liars. I don't think you're trying to con people. I just think that there's something which you're looking for by going out and talking to people. Something truthful. There's no such thing. It's just stories. I'm having no part in it.

I'm done. I'm done. It's done.

He leaves.

Scott, Karl *and* **Simon** *leave.*

Craig *comes back.*

Craig   Last year I was having a stressful day, we were having a barbecue, and Daisy is so like me, she says things that, that I'd say at ten. I, I just started to laugh, thinking it's exactly what I would have said . . . cheeky little shit, but it's exactly what I would have said. So, Daisy was saying something to me about this pack of sausages, going on about it, on about it and she won't eat sausages, she only eats hot dogs. So, I said, they are hot dogs. So, I went and got the, the wrapper out and I said, look, there's the wrapper, hot dogs, yeah but they aren't. I said, Daisy, fuck off. Right, you don't speak to . . . You don't speak to your children like that. So, two hours later before she got ready for a bath I said, I want to have a little chat with you, Daisy. Sit down, yeah. I said, earlier on I said . . . Oh, no, Dad, Dad, Dad, I was annoying you, I was annoying you. I said, look, listen, you don't have to make excuses for what you've said. I said, you . . . I said, the way I spoke to you was unforgivable. Yes, you might have been annoying me but I don't tell you to eff off and, in fact, any adult shouldn't tell you to eff off. She looks at me. I tell you what, Dad, on this occasion I'll forgive you . . .

Methuen Drama Contemporary Dramatists

include

John Arden (two volumes)
Arden & D'Arcy
Peter Barnes (three volumes)
Sebastian Barry
Mike Bartlett
Dermot Bolger
Edward Bond (ten volumes)
Howard Brenton (two volumes)
Leo Butler (two volumes)
Richard Cameron
Jim Cartwright
Caryl Churchill (two volumes)
Complicite
Sarah Daniels (two volumes)
Nick Darke
David Edgar (three volumes)
David Eldridge (two volumes)
Ben Elton
Per Olov Enquist
Dario Fo (two volumes)
Michael Frayn (four volumes)
John Godber (four volumes)
Paul Godfrey
James Graham (two volumes)
David Greig
John Guare
Lee Hall (two volumes)
Katori Hall
Peter Handke
Jonathan Harvey (two volumes)
Iain Heggie
Israel Horovitz
Declan Hughes
Terry Johnson (three volumes)
Sarah Kane
Barrie Keeffe
Bernard-Marie Koltès (two volumes)
Franz Xaver Kroetz
Kwame Kwei-Armah
David Lan
Bryony Lavery
Deborah Levy
Doug Lucie

David Mamet (four volumes)
Patrick Marber
Martin McDonagh
Duncan McLean
David Mercer (two volumes)
Anthony Minghella (two volumes)
Tom Murphy (six volumes)
Phyllis Nagy
Anthony Neilson (two volumes)
Peter Nichol (two volumes)
Philip Osment
Gary Owen
Louise Page
Stewart Parker (two volumes)
Joe Penhall (two volumes)
Stephen Poliakoff (three volumes)
David Rabe (two volumes)
Mark Ravenhill (three volumes)
Christina Reid
Philip Ridley (two volumes)
Willy Russell
Eric-Emmanuel Schmitt
Ntozake Shange
Sam Shepard (two volumes)
Martin Sherman (two volumes)
Christopher Shinn (two volumes)
Joshua Sobel
Wole Soyinka (two volumes)
Simon Stephens (three volumes)
Shelagh Stephenson
David Storey (three volumes)
C. P. Taylor
Sue Townsend
Judy Upton
Michel Vinaver (two volumes)
Arnold Wesker (two volumes)
Peter Whelan
Michael Wilcox
Roy Williams (four volumes)
David Williamson
Snoo Wilson (two volumes)
David Wood (two volumes)
Victoria Wood

Methuen Drama Student Editions

Jean Anouilh *Antigone* • John Arden *Serjeant Musgrave's Dance* • Alan Ayckbourn *Confusions* • Aphra Behn *The Rover* • Edward Bond *Lear* • *Saved* • Bertolt Brecht *The Caucasian Chalk Circle* • *Fear and Misery in the Third Reich* • *The Good Person of Szechwan* • *Life of Galileo* • *Mother Courage and Her Children* • *The Resistible Rise of Arturo Ui* • *The Threepenny Opera* • Anton Chekhov *The Cherry Orchard* • *The Seagull* • *Three Sisters* • *Uncle Vanya* • Caryl Churchill *Serious Money* • *Top Girls* • Shelagh Delaney *A Taste of Honey* • Euripides *Elektra* • *Medea* • Dario Fo *Accidental Death of an Anarchist* • Michael Frayn *Copenhagen* • John Galsworthy *Strife* • Nikolai Gogol *The Government Inspector* • Carlo Goldoni *A Servant to Two Masters* • Lorraine Hansberry *A Raisin in the Sun* • Robert Holman *Across Oka* • Henrik Ibsen *A Doll's House* • *Ghosts* • *Hedda Gabler* • Sarah Kane *4.48 Psychosis* • *Blasted* • Charlotte Keatley *My Mother Said I Never Should* • Bernard Kops *Dreams of Anne Frank* • Federico García Lorca *Blood Wedding* • *Doña Rosita the Spinster* (bilingual edition) • *The House of Bernarda Alba* (bilingual edition) • *Yerma* (bilingual edition) • David Mamet *Glengarry Glen Ross* • *Oleanna* • Patrick Marber *Closer* • John Marston *The Malcontent* • Martin McDonagh *The Lieutenant of Inishmore* • *The Lonesome West* • *The Beauty Queen of Leenane* • Arthur Miller *All My Sons* • *The Crucible* • *A View from the Bridge* • *Death of a Salesman* • *The Price* • *After the Fall* • *The Last Yankee* • *A Memory of Two Mondays* • *Broken Glass* • Percy Mtwa, Mbongeni Ngema and Barney Simon *Woza Albert!* • Joe Orton *Loot* • Joe Penhall *Blue/Orange* • Luigi Pirandello *Six Characters in Search of an Author* • Lucy Prebble *Enron* • Mark Ravenhill *Shopping and F***ing* • Willy Russell *Blood Brothers* • *Educating Rita* • Sophocles *Antigone* • *Oedipus the King* • Wole Soyinka *Death and the King's Horseman* • Shelagh Stephenson *The Memory of Water* • August Strindberg *Miss Julie* • J. M. Synge *The Playboy of the Western World* • Theatre Workshop *Oh What a Lovely War* • Frank Wedekind *Spring Awakening* • Timberlake Wertenbaker *Our Country's Good* • Arnold Wesker *The Merchant* • Oscar Wilde *The Importance of Being Earnest* • Tennessee Williams *A Streetcar Named Desire* • *The Glass Menagerie* • *Cat on a Hot Tin Roof* • *Sweet Bird of Youth*

For a complete listing of
Methuen Drama titles, visit:
www.bloomsbury.com/drama

Follow us on Twitter and keep up to date
with our news and publications
@MethuenDrama